FINANCIAL POINT MAN'S SUCCESS STRATEGIES

VOLUME 4
Estate Planning

William H. Cantrell
CFP®, CLU®

www.cantrellfinancialstrategies.com

ISBN: 978-1482508239

First Printing, February 2013

Published by 102nd Place LLC

Scottsdale, AZ

Printed in the United States of America

Table of Contents

Introduction

My goal in writing this success strategy series is to help interested individuals understand why and how to plan for financial security. The planning I refer to is all about creating wealth and protecting it for yourself and your family. I think most of us can endorse that idea.

We strive to create wealth to be able to enjoy the quality of life we choose. And we certainly care about our family's financial security. And thus it makes perfect sense to have a goal, a purpose, of bringing financial peace of mind to ourself and our family members.

I'm writing this series in Volumes to avoid a "mega-book" that might intimidate or overwhelm readers and keep them from even trying to understand how to move forward in their quest for a better financial life. There are books that take the encyclopedic approach. "Everything you could ever need to answer in your financial life in one easy to read 600 page "publication." If that's right for you then by all means go for it. But typically I find that most people are interested in financial planning in stages based on where they are in their life and how much knowledge they already have about particular topics.

The Internet and our rapidly changing global lifestyle make it difficult for a written document to remain relevant if it tries to be the ultimate source for every question. Better to describe important concepts, practices and tools that have stood the test of time than compute your retirement nest egg amount based on last year's tax rates and stock market performance. Writing the series allows me to update quickly as new information becomes relevant and avail-able.

Volume 1 gives the reader a sense of how broad the Wealth Planning topic is; why it is so big, and some of the crucial questions that need to be answered to create financial peace of mind. Subsequent volumes explore important topics in more detail and allow for updates as history changes our knowledge and strategies.

In each volume I write about what I see as some of the major benefits that come from building a wealth protection plan. Then later in each one I discuss how to go about it. It's much easier to focus on the intricacies of wealth planning after becoming committed to the benefit of doing so.

Here in Volume 4 my focus is on Estate Planning; understanding what you can do to prepare for protecting and sharing your assets during your lifetime and at your death. This is such a vital part of your overall wealth planning. The benefits for you and your loved ones can't be overstated. The end result of proper planning is assets for you during your lifetime and the best possible (lowest cost, easiest, most timely) transfer to your desired beneficiaries.

The second part of this volume looks at issues that confront the spouse or family member who is settling an estate without proper planning. Regrettably, most people don't plan, so most estates are settled by someone facing a difficult task. This section will help to guide that person.

Whether you are preplanning your estate or dealing with an estate after someone's death, I encourage you to get professional advice. We *are* talking about your financial future or a loved one's. Isn't that worth investing in someone to improve YOUR opportunity for success?

Specialists in estate planning are at least as important as your primary care physician. It is rare that you will not benefit from hiring a financial advisor, estate attorney or other specialists such as accountants, realtors, and insurance agents.

I hope you find this book helpful as an aid to you in a time of need. Bereavement counselors have suggested that organizing and settling your finances can be a significant step in the grieving process. If you have lost a loved one recently, you face a tremendous challenge. Not only are you dealing with the pain of loss, but at the same time handling an almost endless array of financial matters.

My last words of advice—don't expect to do it all on schedule and without error. Allow yourself and others the grace of making mistakes, becoming confused or frustrated, and accept that time will enable the process of healing to be accomplished.

I wish you the best for your health, financial and otherwise.

Bill Cantrell

PART ONE

THE ESTATE PLAN

You Can't Take It with You So Now What?

How often have we heard the old adage you can't take it with you? For some people that makes estate planning easy – if I can't take it with me, then I'll just spend it all before I go. The trouble with that philosophy is that most people don't have a clue when they're going to die. And because they don't have a clue, they can't spend it all before they go since they need some of it to live on for as long as they stay on this side of the ground.

Which simply means that estate planning is necessary for everyone, regardless of how much or how little you have when your number is finally up. In its most basic form, Estate Planning is a process used to help you preserve and manage your assets during your lifetime and conserve and distribute them at your death according to your wishes. Because this process is about your assets and your wishes, estate planning can be very different from individual to individual. Ultimately the goals are the same; protect, conserve, manage, and transfer your wealth efficiently and effectively. The ultimate goal is to establish peace of mind for everyone involved.

So let's begin by thinking about our own situation. What would bring peace of mind to you? The answer to that question is a function of who you are. Your health, age, wealth, life goals, lifestyle and other factors will affect how you define what will bring you peace of mind.

What would you need to know or need to have to be at peace about your finances? Although the answer to this question may be a lengthy list, let's start with a small step. Think for a moment and write down three questions you want answered to help you move toward financial success as it relates to protecting, managing and transferring your assets. Just do your top three for now. I want you to get used to thinking in bite-sized pieces. We can't eat an elephant all at once and we can't plan an estate all at once either.

1. _____

2. _____

3. _____

Maybe your questions are basic like what is the difference between a will and a trust? Or, who will get my assets if I die without a will? Or, how do I make sure my kids get my money instead of my ex-spouse?

Or maybe they are more complex like, I want to know how to leave money to my kids, charities and family, but not all at once to my kids who might not be ready to handle a large inheritance. Or, I want to know how to make sure I'm getting the right amount from Social Security now that my spouse has passed, because that is almost all I have to live on.

The role I play with all of my clients is that of their *Financial Point Man*. The person who helps develop the big picture by asking and answering the right questions. Then repeatedly serves to coordinate the client and all of his or her other key advisors (accountants, attorneys, bankers) when appropriate. The lack of an advisor can be costly in many ways, which I'll demonstrate to you throughout the remainder of this book.

Estate Planning Process

As with most things worth having in life, Estate Planning doesn't just happen. The benefit you reap by being proactive in your planning is to ensure your money lasts a lifetime and more.

Who wants to worry at what point you are going to run out? I'm sure you know someone who has had to curtail their lifestyle or return to work at an undesirable age to avoid poverty. Do you know how much you can spend throughout life and not put yourself in jeopardy of running out?

Understanding YOUR particular life situation is vital to prudent planning. And prudent planning is crucial to building financial security.

In the next five chapters I've outlined the steps that will result in a complete, current estate plan. If you take the steps to create and protect your wealth, you'll certainly improve your chance for a less stressful life. It's a result of feeling more in control. Control of current day-to-day events and control of what unforeseeable events might lie ahead.

I have found over the years that answering the questions that most people want answered like, "how much money will I need to settle my estate or how do I make sure my spouse and I are financially secure at end of life?" requires answering many related questions. Thus the role I play with my clients is helping them frame the relevant questions and then doing the work to get meaningful answers.

Protecting your wealth is a continuous project, just like filing a tax return annually and visiting your family physician regularly. Your financial situation is ever changing. Estate planning needs ongoing attention to make sure it is current and complete.

Because there are so many topics and questions with answers which are often not precisely knowable, most people spend very little time trying to do the thinking, planning, and doing that is necessary to accomplish wealth protection. Sort of like building a house when you've never held a hammer - much of the process may seem rather frustrating or confusing. My goal is to motivate you to take the next step, even though you realize you can't accomplish everything at once. It's just too important to ignore completely!

Step 1 – Interview and Hire Your Advisors

I believe strongly that a team of advisors will make all the difference in the ease of completion and success of your estate plan. This team should be multi-disciplined.

A financial planner is a valuable member of the team. The planner's role is to be your guide, your constant companion on the estate planning journey. A good planner will coordinate your planning project with the other team members.

Planners may come with a variety of specialties; insurance, investments, taxes, or general planning. Depending on the planner's specialization, other professionals may be added to the team on an ad hoc basis to ensure all the bases are covered.

You also need an estate attorney who will create the legal documents and act as your ultimate resource for state and national laws to which your plan must adhere.

Often I hear people say they don't know an attorney to go to for estate planning. Or they aren't sure what to ask, what to be prepared to tell, or what to expect from a meeting with an attorney.

And cost is often a puzzle. We have heard of someone who completed an estate plan for a few hundred dollars. And yes, we have heard of others who spent more than a few thousand dollars to get their plan done. Why the difference? And who has the better plan?

No one can know the benefit of a plan or the quality of it simply by knowing the price. Benefit comes in many shapes and sizes and is ultimately measured during the lifetime the plan exists.

Who knows whether your life will go smoothly and you'll never need help from those you select to be your advocates? Or maybe you'll be disabled and require someone to manage your financial and medical care.

Regardless your life situation, interview financial advisors or attorneys until you find a good fit for your taste. Someone who you can believe in their knowledge and trust their judgment. Nothing is more important than finding advisors you trust. Most advisors have advisors in other professions to whom they can refer their clients. Find one advisor and let them help you find the others you need.

I suggest starting with a financial advisor because they are used to gathering all the information—verbal and written—which will help you see where you are financially.

When they are the right advisor, they will help you think through your other estate issues, which will save you time and money when meeting with other professionals.

Step 2 – Gather the Important Facts

Our goal is to protect, conserve, manage and transfer your assets. To do this well we need to know who you are and what is important to you.

For example, we need to know what we have to work with. What do you own and/or owe and what form is it in? Gathering this information is done by creating a financial statement. A sample format for a financial statement called the Statement of Personal Assets and Liabilities is shown on page 89.

In addition to the "real assets" like bank accounts, investments and company retirement accounts that we show in the Financial Statement, we need to include our insurance programs, particularly life insurance as part of our important facts.

Life insurance is an asset "in waiting." Generally it becomes available to your beneficiaries at your death. However, if it is a cash value policy, a portion of your death benefit may be able to be withdrawn prior to your actual passing and used during your lifetime.

Life insurance is an important part of our fact gathering. One of the key questions in Estate Planning is to whom will we leave our wealth. And life insurance gives us several beneficiary designation choices. We can leave our insurance proceeds to pretty much anyone or anything we want. There is no limit to the number of people or charities or organizations or pets we can name.

We'll look at life insurance several times in this Volume, because it can play so many roles. The "facts" about life insurance include: Who is the insured? What is the amount? Who is the beneficiary? Who owns the policy?

As we plan our estate distribution we want to pay special attention to our beneficiary designations. As our life unfolds, as our family grows or shrinks, as our passions change and evolve, it's important to make sure we keep our beneficiary designations current.

To complicate matters, life insurance, annuities, and retirement plans all have their own unique beneficiary designation paperwork. They Do Not follow the traditional estate document selections. This means you cannot make a will or trust and expect decisions that are documented there to apply to insurance policies, annuities and retirement plans *unless* you make the trust the beneficiary.

A key role that I play with my clients, and your financial advisor should play with you, is to be the "point man" on beneficiary designations.

Another critical part of fact gathering is listing the vital information for all family members who are relevant to our planning. This could include spouses, ex-spouses, children, step-children, parents and siblings just to name a few. Before we can begin to make plans for passing our assets on we need to understand the potential beneficiaries:

- Who are they?

- How old are they?
- What is their relationship to us?
- Are there any special considerations regarding their mental or physical health?

Step 3 – Define Your Goals

After gathering the factual information you will want to think about your goals in creating this plan. Your estate attorney will usually have a questionnaire and a process for helping you formulate goals.

I like to do this with my clients before we ever talk with their attorney. It's helpful, and cost effective, to have the facts and the goals thought through preliminarily and then let the attorney add his ideas and guide us on how to accomplish them legally.

Goal setting can be a combination of what you want to have happen and what you want to make sure <u>does not</u> happen with your assets. Although this part of the process is as varied as our personal wishes, there are some basic questions to consider.

- In the simplest way of thinking, who would you like to inherit your wealth? You can give as much or as little to anyone you choose as long as you don't violate any regulations. (An example would be those regulations that require retirement assets to go to your spouse unless he/she agrees ahead of time and signs paperwork to that effect.)

- Do you want to give your assets outright all at once or would you like to set up some ground rules for when beneficiaries can receive some or all of their inheritance? This consideration allows you to protect your beneficiaries in several ways. You may be able to shelter your assets from your beneficiary's creditors or divorcing spouses depending on the laws and practices in your state. Also, you can prevent a beneficiary from spending a sizable inheritance foolishly by specifying under what conditions money may be used

In addition to answering these two basic questions you need to consider if certain assets will be given to specific beneficiaries. For example, you might choose to give retirement assets to your spouse, life insurance to your children, and certain investments to charities. These decisions can be made with the guidance of knowledgeable advisors once the questions above have been answered.

Goal setting is a crucial part of estate planning. Think of it as helping to define the game you are playing. Your advisors need to know what is most important to you to be able to advise you on the best strategy to accomplish your goals.

Step 4 - Analyze the Facts and Make Suggestions

This step is where your advisors do the heavy lifting. You have helped them to this point by providing the factual information (financial and otherwise) and by deciding on your most important goals. Now it's time to determine how easily your goals can be met.

Because I don't know your goals it's difficult for me to make suggestions as to how to accomplish them in this book. What I can do is give you some ideas for meeting your goals under various situations, then you and your advisors can decide if they fit.

If you anticipate spending most of your money during your lifetime and still want to leave a financial legacy you may want to leave the proceeds from a life insurance policy to your beneficiaries.

For those of you who anticipate surplus wealth, you may want to consider "gifting" assets during your lifetime. This allows you and your beneficiaries to enjoy wealth while you are still alive. It also has the added benefit of letting you see how your "gift" gets used.

In another scenario you may be concerned about your loved one's ability to live comfortably after your passing. In this case you will want to examine closely how much money will be needed and what can be done to produce that amount. This might include adding life insurance on your life; reducing spending patterns now so there will not be so much needed at your passing; and saving more so you will have a bigger nest egg to transfer at your death.

The end result of this preliminary analysis is a determination as to how realistic your goals are and where changes might be necessary. This phase will also uncover any special assets; investments, real estate or a family business for example, that may be more complicated to pass to heirs.

Your advisors will be able to help you see potential problems that you might not know about. Some examples are:

1. Potential significant taxes or other expenses in distributing your assets.

2. Lack of liquidity – a majority of assets tied up in a business, real estate or farmland, but very little assets that you can write a check against to cover immediate expenses. This is another place where life insurance proceeds can be instrumental in meeting your estate transfer goals.

Step 5 – Finalize Your Plan

Your effort to this point in the estate planning process is worth very little if you don't take the actions necessary to complete your plan. This can involve any number of tasks, but will almost certainly include signing documents. It may also include purchasing insurance and/or repositioning or retitling assets.

Although it would be great to lay out exactly what you need to do at this point in the process, the actions you need to take are based on the facts and circumstances of your situation. Once again the value of your advisor team is highest when they are helping you understand what actions are necessary to complete your plan and staying engaged with you until the plan is finished.

Even though your specific plan can't be described in this or any book, there are several components that are commonly included or at least considered for inclusion. The purpose of this book is to help you understand:

- The importance of estate planning

- How to go about creating a plan

- The most common components of a plan

With that in mind let me list the five items that I think are the most important for you to understand when building your plan. They are: Wills, Powers of Attorney, Trusts, Letter to Representative and Advanced Directives.

Will

A will is a legal declaration of your wishes as to the transfer of your assets at your death. It also defines the selection of a person or persons (executor) to handle the administration of your estate.

A will can also include who you wish to have guardianship over minor or disabled children. Everyone should have a will regardless of the value of your assets or whether you have other estate documents.

Often people say to me, "I have a Trust, why do I need a Will? or I have a Will, why do I need a Trust?" A will can be the document that governs the transfer for any assets that are not specified in other beneficiary documents such as life insurance policies, annuities and retirement plans. Trusts can serve so many purposes in your estate plan, because they are so versatile. We'll discuss Trusts and their specific role in greater detail a little later.

Powers of Attorney (POA)

A POA is a document in which you give a person(s) the authority (power) to act on your behalf. These documents serve many purposes. The most commonly created POAs are Health Care POA and Durable POA (for financial or business matters).

The Health Care POA is also known as the Medical POA. This document is activated only if you are unable to communicate your own decisions due to incapacity or incom- petence. This is an important protection for you. The actions doctors, hospitals and other health care providers are willing or required to take vary according to state regulations unless a Medical POA is in force.

The POA can be structured to give your agent, also known as an "attorney-in-fact," broad powers or very narrow ones. Generally a Health Care POA will authorize your agent to make decisions regarding your health care when one or more physicians certify that you are not capable of understanding or communicating decisions for yourself.

A Medical or Health Care POA does not cover decisions which are specifically defined in your Living Will, another vital document that everyone should have.

Durable Power of Attorney

A Durable Power of Attorney allows your agent to act on your behalf to conduct business and financial matters. This POA may "spring" into authorization upon the occurrence of a specific event (you become incapacitated) or may be "durable" allowing your agent to act on your behalf at any time.

It is important to consult with your attorney regarding the words that are necessary in your state to allow or restrict your agent to act in the way you desire. An example might be to require a medical doctor to certify that you are incapacitated before your attorney-in-fact can act for you.

Because we are living longer our mental health is more at risk of becoming compromised. Durable Mental Health Care POAs have started cropping up to deal with this issue.

The **Durable Mental Health Care POA** authorizes a mental health professional (psychiatrist or psychologist) to determine if you are incapable of making mental health decisions for yourself. You are able to specify which decisions your agent can make on your behalf.

Examples might be:

- agree to the use of certain medications

- decide to admit you to a treatment facility

- receive information and discuss treatment options with your medical professionals

Letter to Representative (Agent) and Family Letter

These are two important although optional documents. The Letter to Representative acknowledges your wish to designate them to act in some capacity on your behalf. It often times will name an alternate. This could be regarding financial matters or matters of mental or physical health.

The letter will lay out your instructions and expectations so your representative will know in advance what they are agreeing to do for you. If they don't feel they can or want to fulfill your wishes then the letter gives them the opportunity to inform you of their concerns so that you can appoint another person to the position.

The Family Letter makes a wonderful gesture on your behalf. A simple letter is non-binding but with it you can give instructions to your family regarding your choices for burial, memorial services and other personal matters that you know may concern them.

This is especially valuable if you know or anticipate there may be different opinions among family members as to what should be done. A family letter can ease the burden on survivors and allow your wishes to be met.

Living Will

A living will has become such an important part of every estate plan. It is your opportunity to share your wishes with family and medical professionals in the event you become unable to communicate.

The living will is used if you are in a coma or a persistent vegetative state and want to authorize or refuse treatment that is designed to prolong your life.

You may state your wishes to your primary physician or an alternate. You may also state under what scenarios your living will can be invoked. For example, you may require two medical doctors to agree on your terminal condition before the living will is applicable.

Most times a spouse or other family member does not want to decide on withdrawing or extending life sustaining treatment. Your wishes are paramount in this situation and yet you are unable to let your wishes be known through normal communication.

Make sure you have a living will document! And thereby assure your loved ones about your preference and allow them and your medical team to honor your desires.

Do Not Resuscitate (DNR)

This legal order is written by a medical professional after consultation with the patient and/or the Health Care POA. It allows the medical team to "permit natural death" to occur rather than using CPR or other cardiac life support if you were to stop breathing or go in to cardiac arrest.

A DNR does not prevent any other treatment and is commonly considered by patients who are elderly, with multiple medical problems, or advanced cancers and are unlikely to survive such a situation.

Trusts

Probably the most versatile estate document is a trust. There are various types and myriad reasons for why you might want to use a trust. The most common type is called a Revocable Living Trust.

It is important to remember that the goal of estate planning is to arrange for the management and transfer of your assets in the event or your death or incapacity. Most people think about estate planning relating to their death only. However, the beauty of a trust is that it can be the guiding document allowing someone of your choosing to manage your assets on YOUR behalf if you are unable to do so due to disability or incapacity.

Using a trust allows you to select a manager and give guidance as to when and how you wish that person to act in managing and/or transferring your assets.

One of the most important features of a <u>Revocable Trust</u> is that it can be modified, even cancelled, for as long as you are alive. Thus any decision you make (the beneficiaries, who gets what assets, when they receive them, who manages the assets on your behalf, etc.) and anything you put in your trust can be changed whenever you desire.

In my experience, people are apt to shy away from trusts. The most prevalent concerns seem to be:

1. Cost – people expect a trust to be more costly than the benefit they see getting from having one. I have seen attorneys charge less than $1000 for a trust and I have seen

essentially the same trust billed at $5000. Unfortunately, this is what leads to the perception that trusts are expensive. It isn't always clear what creates the value in one trust versus another.

2. The three Cs: Complicated, Complex, Cumbersome – Often I've heard individuals say they think a trust is more complicated and difficult to work with i.e. the language, the decisions needed, the responsibilities of executors, the restrictions on beneficiaries' use, etc.

When can beneficiaries access funds? What can they use the money for? Who has ultimate say in managing the investment of the assets?

After talking with a competent attorney who will take the time to explain the value and the operational aspects of a trust I find most people are much more inclined to use one.

Trust benefits are numerous. Think again about our goal in estate planning – protect, conserve, manage and transfer assets. A Revocable Trust can address each of these topics.

On my top five list of benefits that a trust provides are these:

1. You know your affairs are in order and your wishes can be carried out.

2. Your family is not burdened by the uncertainty of how to manage or transfer your assets.

3. Minor children and/or other bene-ficiaries can be provided for in the way you wish until they are able to manage affairs on their own.

4. Assets may be protected from your beneficiaries' creditors.

5. A trust maintains the privacy of your estate plan assets.

Part One - Summary

An Estate Plan is a wonderful gift to give yourself and your loved ones. Remember the plan is for you if you need help during your lifetime and honors your wishes for your beneficiaries at your passing.

A complete plan will include at a minimum a Will, Durable Power of Attorney, Health Care Power of Attorney, and Living Will.

It may also include one or more types of trusts.

So do yourself and your family a favor and get your Estate Plan completed!

PART TWO

WHEN IT FALLS TO YOU

Death Has Come, Now What?

It's time to settle your loved one's estate. Do they have a current, complete estate plan? Or were they one of the 55% of individuals living in America who never created a will let alone a complete estate plan?

The statistics are sad, but true. Recent numbers suggest that as high as 75% of certain nationalities in this country die without a simple will. I've spent the first eight chapters of this book trying to explain the "how and the why" of estate planning. But I know there is a major part of my audience that needs to know what to do and how to do it when someone they know dies without a will.

So here's goes. It's called "intestate," dying with no estate plan, including no will. At this point the laws of the state in which the deceased resided take over.

First an administrator is appointed by the probate court in the county of jurisdiction. The court is responsible for supervising the legal process by which all financial affairs of people who die in that county are settled.

This can be pretty straight forward if there is a surviving spouse or child who can be appointed. The further removed family members are geographically and/or in lineage, the more cumbersome this process can become.

The role of the court appointed ad-ministrator is similar to the role of executor if one had been chosen through a trust or will. Both individuals will need to do the proper documenting and reporting to the court regarding the completion of the deceased's financial affairs and the distribu-tion of their assets.

The Surviving Spouse

Although not having a will at your death means the courts are more involved in settling your estate, a bigger concern for me is the stress, confusion and possible heartache that not having a will can cause for your loved ones. So let's focus on the impact to the surviving spouse, and perhaps other beneficiaries who might be significantly impacted by your passing.

I'm going to write from the point of view of the surviving spouse who is likely the most materially affected. Other beneficiaries may have similar concerns or issues but they will usually be less than the spouse's.

The stress of a death comes from the grief, uncertainty, new responsibilities, and the need to pay attention to urgent matters all while you are trying to get your bearings as a "single" person instead of a couple, a team. Now imagine adding to that situation the disarray your finances may be in without an estate plan. You have to press ahead to try to figure it out. There's nothing else you can do and unfortunately, you are the only one who can do some of the work.

So now what? Start simply is my advice. Make a list of your most pressing concerns. On pages 66 through 83 you'll find a list of 14 that I think are commonly at the top of most people's lists. But your 3, 5, 10 or 14 issues are what really matter to you.

The ones I list should help to make sure nothing falls through the cracks but your team of advisors (put this team in place now if you didn't build it prior to your loved one's death) will become invaluable as you work through your new financial life.

Some general thoughts for you:

- Make your list of concerns. Even if you feel you don't really know much about your financials, that list tells you and your advisors what state of mind you are in regarding money. This is very important. As an advisor I want to know if you are knowledgeable, confident, disinterested, scared, or whatever, and the list of concerns can help.

- Go slowly but consistently. There will rarely be too many things to do if you do a little every day. Set a time and place if you don't already have a routine. Keep complete notes and records. If files are not set up or available to you, create your own. Page 91 has a list of possible file names. Pick those that best fit your situation and add others.

- Start by answering the questions, "What do I own?" and "What do I owe?" The answers to those two simple questions will outline for you the big picture. Is there a lot of wealth and a little debt or just the opposite? The Statement of Personal Assets and Liabilities on page 89 is a handy worksheet to summarize this information.

- Use the Cash Needs Worksheet on page 93 as a tool for gathering more detailed information about how your money is spent. The Immediate Cash Resources section of the worksheet is divided into cash that is immediately available in the next 30 days and cash that you expect to be available within 90 days. Completing this worksheet allows you, and your advisors, to know a great deal about where you are getting money. Similarly, if the majority of this page is blank or unknown then there is much more work to be done.

The same is true for the Immediate Cash Requirements section of the worksheet. List the bills you know about or can reasonably assume you'll need to pay within the next 30 to 90 days. Most creditors will understand a brief delay while you get your financial house in order.

- Another valuable form is the Important Document Location Checklist on page 99. If you are fortunate you will have a file or files for some of the documents on this list. If you are not so fortunate you will need to hunt them down as you go through the settling of your spouse's estate. As you gather the documents, you should MAKE COPIES of them and complete the checklist that tells you, and others, where they may be found. A word of caution, NO vital document (will, trust, birth or marriage certificate) should be kept only in your safe deposit box unless your attorney or POA agent knows this and has access to the box. Again, the checklist helps keep you organized and can help keep others informed.

Now let's think about potentially important sources of income or assets where you may need to take action in order to receive them.

Life Insurance
Life insurance can come from many sources i.e. your employer, your spouse's employer, personal policies taken out by you or your spouse, union or professional associations, AARP, and Social Security. All are possibilities.

This "project" of finding out what you actually have in life insurance can take some digging. You may have to sort through bank statements to see who is getting paid. It may be contacting the agencies, organizations and employers to discover what is available to you. Without question this search is worth it!

When you do locate policies on your deceased spouse's life, make sure you ask what documentation is required to receive the proceeds. Also find out what options are available for payment other than taking the money in a lump sum. Most insurance companies will offer a payment over several years and will pay you interest on the funds you leave with them. This is another example of where your financial advisor can be instrumental in helping you learn about options and their impact on your situation. Based on the cash requirements you identified earlier, you may need all of the proceeds immediately or you may be better served to invest a portion of them.

Finally, life insurance proceeds may take several weeks to receive. Insurance companies understandably have a due diligence process to which they must adhere. If there appear to be any abnormalities in the circumstances surrounding the death the process can be delayed.

Medical Insurance

Even more important than checking on life insurance proceeds is making sure you know the status of medical insurance coverage. If your coverage was through your spouse's employer you may need to arrange other coverage or begin to pay the premiums yourself if that is allowed.

The Federal law known as COBRA allows you to maintain your existing coverage in most cases up to 36 months after your spouse's death. In terms of knowing what resources you have and what bills you need to pay, health insurance is at the very top of the list.

Investment and Employer Retirement Accounts

Your other sources for assets are in your personal investment accounts, i.e. bank accounts, investments, personal retirement accounts such as IRAs and annuities, and in your spouse's employer 401K, deferred income or pension plan(s).

Some employers offer employees an opportunity to save for retirement through a 401K or similar plan. It used to be that the employer would fully fund a "pension" plan for an employee's retirement years. That approach became much less common beginning in the late 1980s.

If you contact your spouse's Human Resources department they will be able to give you the information about all benefits you have available – life, health, and disability insurances, retirement pay in any form, vacation pay or sick pay that is owed to your spouse and anything that might be a special benefit at their company.

Social Security

The benefits available through Social Security vary depending on several factors such as your age, the age of your unmarried children, whether children or other dependents are disabled and other combinations of factors. This is a complex area which may have far reaching implications to you.

Although you will need to meet with Social Security staff to provide information and documentation and ultimately to learn from them your options for receiving payments, I urge you to work with a properly trained financial advisor and/or attorney before you make any decisions. Get in touch with your local Social Security office and get **IN WRITING** your benefit options as they explained them to you.

I attend these meetings with my clients if at all possible. At a minimum I review all the information before my client signs anything. It's too important not to give it this level of attention.

"Will Social Security be there for me?" is another consideration. I believe the answer is yes. It is too well embedded in the fabric of our Country's entitlement package, particularly for the elderly, disabled and surviving immediate family. It will change certainly, retirement age and amount probably, and the same for disability. But in my opinion it will be a part of our legacy for many, many years to come.

Acting on the Information

By now we have looked at the most important parts of our financial picture. We want to understand what is most critical to us if we are suddenly forced to take over the settlement of our Spouse's estate and making all the financial decisions.

As a reminder, that means we need to know how much we own, how much we owe, what form our "owned assets" are in, what do we have to do to be able to use them, and how long before they will be at our disposal. If we've completed the Cash Needs Worksheet on page 93 we will have learned what we need to know.

Now we can begin to answer questions and take action on those things that are foremost in our mind. Questions that

65

family, friends, advisors and sales professionals may want us to answer.

I want to go back to my 14 most important questions and see how you might answer, now that you know what resources you have and what obligations you need to be ready to pay.

Financial Position:

Question 1 – What should I do right now? And Question 2 – Should I, and if so how do I, choose a financial advisor?

Any decisions you make, i.e. go to work, stop working, continue with your present status, are best made after a little time of rest and rejuvenation. These decisions should not be made in the midst of your period of mourning.

Going through the mourning process is tough, emotional work. It will sap your energy and occupy your best thinking. So avoid any important decisions if at all possible at this time.

You will want the help of your financial advisor to compile, analyze and project your overall financial picture before you begin making decisions that will have a lasting impact.

The 12 remaining questions that I suggest could well be at the top of your list of concerns are answered much more easily (and I believe accurately) with guidance from an advisor who is trained to look holistically at your situation.

Ideally that advisor is someone you know and trust before you need help in this serious situation. If not, finding the right person will take a tremendous load off your shoulders.

Question 3 – Do I have enough money for immediate needs?

If you do the worksheets starting on page 93 you should be able to answer this vital question. You *must* know the answer to understand whether or not you are in financial crisis. No one is in such crisis that their financial matters can't be handled. But knowing the facts will allow you to get the right kind of help from your advisors.

Question 4 – Will I have enough income to live comfortably without working?

The Cash Flow Worksheet on page 101 is the tool to use to help you discover the answer. Get that monthly budget done! Decide what you must have monthly to pay your obligations. A realistic budget means you will have some left over for fun or emergencies. You are not a robot and you don't have perfect control over what you will need to spend monthly. Fun money has probably never been more important than during a time of grief. And an emergency fund speaks for itself.

Protection

Question 5 – What about medical coverage?

The place to start with medical insurance is to know (or find out) how you are presently covered. Check with your spouse's employer if your spouse had family insurance through his/her work. If you had your own coverage through your employer, Medicare, or another arrangement not much should need to be changed. However, you may need to remove your spouse from your plan.

Without being redundant let me just say the decision around medical insurance need and type is best sorted out with a professional. One of the really positive aspects of our evolving world is that we have so many choices in life.

Of course with the additional choices come features and nuances that allow us to make what we opt for more tailored to our own unique situation. These differences add complexity to the products and services we are buying. Sometimes those complexities mean very little to us and sometimes they are critically important.

For example, do you want comprehensive major medical insurance with a $500 deductible or a policy with a $10,000 deductible that acts as more of a catastrophic coverage plan? These two options will be very different in price. If the question I pose sounds like gobbledygook then you understand why getting help in making insurance decisions is necessary.

Question 6 – Will there be enough money to last, even if I need long-term health care at some point?

The need for long-term health care service is becoming more common as we live longer. In 1960 our average life expectancy was 69.77 years according to the World Bank. In the 50 years since then it has increased to 78.24 years. That's almost 10 years longer!

A man turning 65 in 2013 can expect to live until the age of 83; a woman until age 85. One out of four of us will live to age 90 and one out of ten will live past age 95 according to the Social Security Administration. www.ssa.gov

Consequently, we need to be much more concerned about how we will pay for the services we may need in our later years. Medical care and life care have become a tremendous expense for us and the agencies in our society that support the elderly and infirmed.

For most of us long-term care insurance is an option which should be considered strongly. If we are concerned about not being forced to use our assets, including possibly the equity in our home, we will need to have an insurance policy to cover some or all of the additional life care expenses we may incur. You should plan on $50,000 to $80,000 per year if you need comprehensive care. The lower amount would apply to significant services provided in your home or an assisted living facility with the higher amount representing what it might cost in a nursing home.

The real point is that this is big money and most people can't afford to pay it out of their own savings/investment accounts. Medicare pays only a limited amount and only for a few days. Medicaid only pays after your own financial resources have been exhausted. Neither is a great option making long-term care insurance even more valuable.

As an aside, long-term care insurance is getting harder to acquire as some insurers leave the market and others raise premiums and underwriting requirements.

Question 7 – Should I have (or change) life insurance?

The answer to this question is subject to many factors, but the decision to own life insurance usually comes down to one of four situations.

- If you have anyone dependent on your income or assets for their financial well-being. If your passing would eliminate financial resources others will need to live comfortably, then you should consider insurance to replace some or all of this potential loss.
- If your debts would be a burden to your heirs because you do not have enough assets to pay them off at your death. Most people will not want to leave unpaid bills. Particularly if the debts were "jointly" owned with someone such as a home mortgage with your spouse. You might want enough insurance to at least pay off your half.
- If you want to make certain you can leave an inheritance to someone or a bequest to a charity, you may want to use life insurance to handle all or a portion of that amount. This is becoming more common when there are second marriages. Children or step-children are receiving life in-

surance proceeds and the surviving spouse is receiving all or a major part of the real money assets.

- If you have significant need for cash relatively quickly after your loved one's passing, life insurance can be a smart way to deal with that need. This situation can occur if you have a sizable estate and expect to owe estate taxes. Another possible reason would be you own a business or real estate with a partner and need cash to buy out the partner or to continue operating. The Worksheet on page 105 will help you understand how you might determine your need for life insurance.

Question 8 – How should I invest life insurance proceeds? and Question 9 – What should I do with 401(K), IRA and company pension funds?

The answer to these questions is part of a bigger question. How much do you have in total to invest i.e. life insurance proceeds, retirement plans, IRAs, non-retirement investments, bank checking, savings and CD accounts? And how much of that money do you need in the next 1, 3, 5 or 10 years?

Most people who need money a year from now want to know it will be there for them. Hence, they may want to take little or no risk in investing that money. Consequently, they will take little or no return just to know that there is no risk of loss.

Funds that are not needed for several years are viewed differently. Depending on a person's willingness to see the value in their account rise and fall, assets can be invested for greater potential return. Usually this is done by selecting a mix of investments that have proven themselves over time to provide an acceptable return.

Your financial advisor will first discuss your tolerance for risk. Risk is normally thought of as the degree of fluctuation in account value in a given period of time. Knowing your risk tolerance, the advisor can build a portfolio of investments, some with no risk, some with greater risk, and others with the most risk you are willing to take. The mixture and the percentage of your assets in each category is purely based on your needs, your willingness to take risk, and the type of investments your advisor provides.

Retirement Planning

Question 10 – Will I have enough for retirement years?

This question is more easily answered if you are already retired or are within 5 to 10 years of retiring. In those situations you pretty much know what your retirement scenario is or is likely to be. You know how much money you have to use, how much you are spending now, and what potential changes will be occurring – perhaps a mortgage or other debt being paid off soon.

If you have a few more years before retirement you can assume you'll increase your account balances modestly, but prudence requires you to choose a low rate (3% to 6%) of increase.

When you know, or have a good idea of, your available income from Social Security or pensions, your investment assets and your current expenses, your advisor can help you project your ability to live the lifestyle you choose in retirement. If the numbers add up the way you want – hurray! If not it is vitally important to make changes. You'll need to reduce your expenses, or look at possibly modifying your investments to take just a little more risk in anticipation of a higher return.

This last option (taking more risk) is the least desirable because there are no guarantees it will occur. Investment return is just a statistic; something to expect over a LONG time. Rarely does the stock market not grow over a 5 to 10 year period but it does happen. Don't expect an unrealistic investment performance to bail out your need for cash. Take matters into your own hands and do what is necessary to create a plan and way of living that gives you financial peace of mind.

Question 11 – When should I plan to take Social Security?

This topic can generate as many options as insurance and almost as much confusion. There are a couple of factors that you should use to help you decide when to take Social Security.

- How badly do you need that monthly amount to balance your budget? The earliest you can take Social Security is age 62 (as of February 2013) on your own work history and age 60 if your spouse is deceased. Note – if you are disabled you may take Social Security at age 50.

- How much is the amount and how much might it be if you wait until full retirement age or even longer? Full retirement age is 65 for people born before 1937. For each year after 1937 your full retirement age increases by 2 months until 1943. Full retirement is age 66 if you were born between 1943 and 1954. It gradually increases by two months per year until it reaches age 67 for people born 1960 and later.

If you take your benefit before full retirement age your monthly amount will be reduced by up to 30% depending on your birth year. For most people the average reduction will be around 25%.

Let's assume your full retirement benefit is $1000 per month. Would you rather get $750 per month at age 62 or wait four to five years and get the full $1000? Many people would say "show me the money" and take it at age 62.

There is absolutely no universally right answer because much of the impact of your choice is beyond anyone's knowledge. For example: How long will you live?

If you die before age 77 you will have been better off taking an earlier payment. If we ignore earnings rates on the money you are receiving and any increases in monthly SSA payments that you might get, it will take twelve years after you begin to get paid to receive as much from Social Security as you do by starting at age 62. In year thirteen and beyond you would technically be ahead by waiting until age 65 to start taking payments.

With all the uncertainties – life expectancy, earnings on your investments, potential for Social Security to be altered in the future – many people will opt for an earlier payment. I can't say I blame them.

On the flip side, Social Security is generally considered a predictable amount that increases every year you don't take it. In fact it increases 8% per year from full retirement age to age 70. So if it works for you to wait until 65, 66 or all the way to age

70, you could have a significantly larger monthly payment.

For example, look at this chart:

Year of Birth	Full Benefit Age	Full Benefit Amount	Benefit at age 62	Benefit at age 70
Before 1938	65	$1,000	$800	$1,400
1943 to 1954	66	$1,000	$750	$1,320
1960 and later	67	$1,000	$700	$1,240

I think I've written enough to give you the idea that this is a complex decision particularly when you look at the variety of options. I haven't even touched on whether you are the ex-spouse of a deceased person or whether there are minor children of the deceased that you are raising. These are two more situations that have their own set of rules regarding your monthly payment. So I strongly encourage you to talk with your advisor and a representative from Social Security before you decide anything.

Estate Preservation

Question 12 – How should my will be changed?

Let's start with the premise that *every* adult needs a will. Whether you have a sizable estate or a very small one, you need a will. It is your opportunity to express your wishes regarding the transfer of your assets at your death.

Even if you think you may not care who receives your assets, your heirs do. If you die without a will your state of residence will have jurisdiction over who receives your property. Often this would not be exactly the way you would choose.

Each state makes their own rules. Some split assets among the spouse and children. Others give a fixed amount i.e. $50,000 to the spouse and split the remainder among the spouse and any other heirs.

If your Will specified that your now deceased spouse was to receive your property at your death then you will need to change your Will. This simply means naming a new person or person(s) to receive your assets when you die.

Equally as important if not more so is the updating of your POA documents if needed. Most people will have a spouse as primary or secondary on their Estate Documents i.e.

Financial and Medical POAs, Living Wills and Trusts. After your spouse's passing you need to consider who should be added, if anyone, in their place. There may have been other changes in your life situation. Perhaps others who you had selected as secondary or tertiary POAs have passed also or moved away and it no longer makes sense to have them involved. Those situations often get ignored when your Primary (your spouse) is alive.

Question 13 – Do I need a Living Will?

A living will is as valuable to you and your family as any document you have. It allows you to communicate your wishes to family and your medical team(s) if you become incapacitated.

Having an incapacitated family member is a stressful situation for everyone. Letting them know your desires about whether to use special treatment to keep you alive if you have been judged to be in a terminal, irreversible medical condition is really valuable and in some jurisdictions may be required for end of life action to be taken. Do you really want to leave decisions about your end of life care to a vote of loving family members, who may have differing views on that very personal topic? Not fair to them and perhaps not what you would have chosen; thus the need for a Living Will.

Question 14 – Do I need a Trust?

Page 47 explained the benefits of using a trust. I believe strongly in the value of a trust and encourage all my clients to consider one.

I like trusts because I think they provide the most flexibility and the most protection for you and your beneficiaries. A trust allows you to decide when someone will receive your assets after your passing. Do they get it all at once or a little at a time, or part now and part later? Also, it may protect your heir's financial solvency if they should need to shelter assets from creditors.

A trust will allow you to choose who will manage your financial matters if you become disabled or incapacitated. Sometimes this can be handled by a spouse, but often a spouse or child does not have the interest or the ability to manage your complete financial affairs. In this situation EVERYONE is better served if you pick the **best** person or company, not just the logical, easiest person.

In Conclusion

Understanding estate planning issues is not easy but it is doable. With a little education and time spent on your part, you can hire a team of professionals who can do the heavy lifting in helping you gather information, set goals, think through the possibilities to meet those goals, and prepare the plans and documents you need. Don't be afraid to ask for help!

The satisfaction you will feel from getting your plan done is huge and the benefit to you and your loved ones is indescribable.

Why not get started today?

All the best,

Bill

PART THREE

FORMS,
WORKSHEETS,
REFERENCES

Statement of Personal Assets and Liabilities

STATEMENT OF PERSONAL ASSETS AND LIABIILITIES

ASSETS	AMOUNT		AMOUNT
PROPERTY		MORTGAGES, EQUITY LINES	
VEHICLES		LOANS ON VEHICLES	
CASH, INVESTMENTS, ETC		OVERDRAWN BALANCES	
FURNITURE, HOUSEHOLD ITEM, JEWELRY, ETC.		PERSONAL LOANS, CREDIT CARDS, ETC.	
OTHER ASSETS		OTHER LIABILITIES	
TOTAL ASSETS		TOTAL LIABILITIES	

SURPLUS/(DEFICIT) ASSETS MINUS LIABILITIES = _____

File Headings

Auto Insurance

Auto Registration

Bank Statements

Birth Certificates

Credit Card Statements

Death Certificates

Health Insurance Information

Income Tax Information

Investment Statements

IRA Statements

Life Insurance Information

Living Wills

Marriage Certificate

Military Discharge Papers

File Headings continued:

Mortgage Statements

Pension Accounts

Powers of Attorney

Property and Casualty Insurance

Real Estate Titles and Deeds

Safe Deposit Box Information

Social Security Records

Title Insurance

Trust Agreements

Wills

401(k) accounts

Cash Needs Worksheet

When a spouse dies it is critical for the surviving spouse or significant other to quickly get a handle on the amount of cash they will need to get by for the first 90 days and where that cash will come from. You can use this easy worksheet to assist you in that process.

Immediate Cash Resources

0 to 30 Days

Name/Source	Amount Available
Checking Accounts:	
1.	$
2.	
3.	
Total	$
Money Market Accounts:	
1.	$
2.	
3.	
Total	$

Savings Accounts:

1. _____ $ _____

2. _____ _____

3. _____ _____

                        Total $ _____

Certificates of Deposit:

1. _____ $ _____

2. _____ _____

3. _____ _____

                        Total $ _____

Investment Income:

1. Dividends $ _____

2. Interest   _____

                        Total $ _____

From Your Spouse's Employer:

1. Wages Due $ _____

2. Vacation Pay   _____

3. Sick Leave Pay   _____

4. Misc. Accrued Pay   _____

5. Disability Payments   _____

                        Total $ _____

From Your Employer:

1. Wages $ _____

2. Bonuses   _____

                        Total $ _____

Total Immediate Cash
 within 0-30 days $ _____

Expected within 90 days

Name/Source	Amount
Life Insurance Proceeds:	
1. _____	$ _____
2. _____	_____
3. _____	_____
Total	$ _____
Retirement Survivor Benefits:	
1. 401(k)	$ _____
2. Pension/Profit Sharing Plan	_____
3. IRA Account(s)	_____
4. Social Security/Gov't. Benefits	_____
5. Previous Employer Pension	_____
Total	$ _____
Cash Value of *Your* Life Insurance	
Policy(ies) Available as Loan or Withdrawal	
1. _____	$ _____
2. _____	_____
Total	$ _____
Spouse's Medical Payment	
Reimbursements:	
1. Medicare	$ _____
2. Private Medical Insurance	_____
Total	$ _____

Miscellaneous:

1. _____ $ _____

2. _____ _____

3. _____ _____

Total $ _____

Total Cash (30-90 Days) $ _____

Total Cash (0-30 Days) $ _____

Total Cash (30-90 Days) _____

Grand Total Cash (0-90 Days) $ _____

Immediate Cash Requirements

Comparing your immediate needs with what you expect to have in the next 90 days keeps you from having to guess where you stand and enables you to plan accordingly.

Item	Due Date	Amount Due
Household Operation		
(1 Month Estimate)	_____	$ _____
Funeral Expenses:		
1.	_____	$ _____
2.	_____	_____
3.	_____	_____
4.	_____	_____
5.	_____	_____
6.	_____	_____
Totals		$ _____
Outstanding Bills Now Due:		
1.	_____	$ _____
2.	_____	_____
3.	_____	_____
4.	_____	_____
5.	_____	_____
6.	_____	_____
7.	_____	_____
8.	_____	_____
9.	_____	_____
Totals		$ _____
Total Expenses (Funeral plus Outstanding Due)		$ _____

Important Document Location Checklist

For ease of use, include account numbers if applicable in the space provided for the location.

File Header/Document Type	Safe Deposit Box	Office	Residence	Other
Bank/Creditor Statements:				
Checking accounts				
Savings accounts				
Cerificates of Deposit				
Credit Cards				
Mortgage loans				
Auto loans				
Home Equity loans				
Student loans				
Insurance:				
Auto policy				
Homeowners policy				
Life policy				
Health policy				
Long-term care policy				
Accident/Disability				
Retirement Plans:				
401(k)				
IRA				
Self-employment plans				
Pension				
Profit sharing				
ESOP				

File Header/Document Type	Safe Deposit Box	Office	Residence	Other
Estate Planning:				
Wills				
Living Wills				
Trusts				
Powers of Attorney				
Social Security Record/Card				
Birth Certificates				
Death Certificates				
Marriage Certificates				
Prenuptial Agreement				
Divorce papers				
Adoption papers				
Investments and Taxes:				
Last two years taxes & documents				
Stock/securities Brokerage 1				
Stock/securities Brokerage 2				
Stock/securities Brokerage 3				
Stock or Bond Certificates				
Personal/Ownership:				
Real Estate title and deeds				
Auto title and registration				
Recreational property title				
Burial plot title				
Burial instructions				
Passports				
Military discharge papers				
Naturalization/citizenship papers				
Uniform Donor card				
Business:				
Partnership agreements				
Articles of Incorporation				
Operating agreement				
Financial books and records				
Employment contracts				
Patents/copyrights				
Other contracts				

Cash Flow Planning Worksheet

Income	Monthly	Annually
Salary/Wages/Distribution	$ _____	$ _____
Interest	_____	_____
Dividends	_____	_____
IRA Income	_____	_____
Annuity Income	_____	_____
Pension Income	_____	_____
Rental Income	_____	_____
Partnership Income	_____	_____
Civil Service Benefits	_____	_____
Child Support/Alimony	_____	_____
Tax Refunds	_____	_____
Bonuses, Gifts	_____	_____
401(k) or 401(b) Income	_____	_____
Other	_____	_____
TOTAL INCOME	$ _____	$ _____

EXPENSES

	Monthly	Annually
Rent/Mortgage	$ _____	$ _____
Property Taxes	_____	_____
Homeowners Assoc. Fees	_____	_____
Home Insurance	_____	_____
Utilities	_____	_____
Services (trash, pool, etc.)	_____	_____
Groceries/supplies	_____	_____

Expenses (continued)	Monthly	Annually
Cleaning		
Cable/Satelite/Phone		
Home Maintenance		
Home Improvements		
Appliances/Repair		
Furniture and Fixtures		
Clothing		
Dry Cleaning/Laundry		
Hair Care/Cosmetics		
Entertainment/Hobbies		
Vacations/Travel		
Education		
Dues/Membership Fees		
Pets/Pet Care		
Charity/Religious Inst.		
Children's Tuition		
Room/Board		
Books and Supplies		
Summer Camp		
Lessons (dance, music, etc)		
Sports Activities/Gyms		
Lunch Money		
Allowance		
Child Care/Babysitter		
Doctors		
Dentists		
Specialists		
Prescription Drugs		
Glasses		

Expenses (continued)	Monthly	Annually
Car Loan/Lease		
Auto Insurance		
Gas/Oil		
Maintenance		
License Fees/Tags		
Life Insurance		
Health Insurance		
Accident/Disability Ins.		
Long-term Care Insurance		
Federal Income Tax		
State/City/Local Income Tax		
Personal Property Tax		
Other		
TOTAL EXPENSES	$	$
List Your Total Income	$	$
Subtract Your Total Expense	-	-
Net Cash Flow Remaining for Savings & Investment	$	$

Life Insurance Need Worksheet

	Your Data	Example
I. Family Income (Yearly)		
a. Monthly cash flow x 12		75,000
b. Minus: Estimated Social Security Benefits		-25,000
c. Minus: Pension		0
d. Minus: Other miscellaneous income		0
e. Equals: Income need from Investment		50,000
f. Investment capital need assuming 4% after tax return (Divide I.e by 4%)		**1,250,000**
II. Debt Fulfillment Needs		
a. Mortgage(s)		350,000
b. Bank loans/lines of credit		10,000
c. Credit card(s)		2,000
d. Miscellaneous		0
e. Total Debt		**362,000**
III. Other Funding Needs		
a. Emergency reserve (at least 90 days)		30,000
b. Cash needed for other goals		50,000
c. Total Other Funding		**80,000**
IV. Estate Settlement Expense		
a. Funeral		10,000
b. Federal Estate Tax if applicable		0
c. State Death Tax if applicable		0
d. Administrator/Probate fees		2,500
e. Medical costs not covered by insurance		2,500
f. Miscellaneous		0
g. Total		**15,000**

	Your Data	Example
V. Summary of Total Capital Needs:		
a. Family Income from I.f		1,250,000
b. Debt Fulfillment Needs from II.e		362,000
c. Other Funding Needs from III.c		80,000
d. Estate Settlement Expense from IV.g		15,000
e. Total		**1,707,000**
VI. Income Producing Assets		
a. Cash and Investments		1,200,000
b. Pension		0
c. 401(k) and/or Profit Sharing Plan		0
d. IRA, Keogh (HR-10)		400,000
e. Life Insurance on your life		100,000
f. Total		**1,700,000**
VII. Capital Need Assessment		
a. Total Capital Need from V.e		1,707,000
b. Minus: Income Producing Assets from VI.f		-1,700,000
c. Net Capital (Insurance) needed		**7,000**

Resources

American Association of Retired Persons
www.aarp.org   800-424-3410

American Institute of Certified Public
Accountants www.aicpa.org 888-777-7077

Consumer Credit Counseling Services
www.cccsintl.org   866-531-3433

Department of Veterans Affairs
www.va.gov   800-827-1000

Estate Planning Attorneys
www.estateplanninglawfirms.com

Financial Advisors
www.cfp.net   800-487-1497

Internal Revenue Service
www.irs.gov

Medicare and Medigap
www.medicare.gov   800-633-4227

National Association of Personal Financial
Advisors   www.napfa.org   847-483-5400

Social Security Administration
www.ssa.gov   800-772-1213

Bibliography

Bennett, Jarratt G, and Lorry M. Ciporkin. *Making the Money Last: Financial Clarity for the Surviving Spouse*. Fairfax: Bennett Publications, 2003.

Domini, Amy L. with Dennis Pearne and Sharon L. Rich. *The Challenges of Wealth: Mastering the Personal and Financial Conflicts*. Homewood, Illinois: Dow Jones-Irwin, 1988.

Esperti, Robert A. and Renno L. Peterson with Willard A. Johnson. *Generations: Planning Your Legacy*. Denver: Esperti Peterson Institute Incorporated, 1999.

Graves, Edward E. *McGill's Life Insurance*. Bryn Mawr, PA: The American College, 2009.

Hogan, Paul and Lori Hogan. *Stages of Senior Care: Your Step-by-Step Guide to Making the Best Decisions.* New York: McGraw Hill, 2010.

Kurlowicz, Ted. *Estate Planning Applications.* Bryn Mawr, PA: The American College, 2006.

About the Author

Bill Cantrell is a financial coach with over thirty years in the financial services industry. As a Registered Investment Advisor he specializes in providing a full range of planning and coaching services that are tailored to each individual's specific needs. He won't **just** manage your investments, he won't **just** give you the best insurance options, and he won't **just** help you avoid paying more taxes than you should. Bill does all of that and more. Everything in fact that's needed to ensure you reach your goals.

Bill is a CFP® (Certified Financial Planner) and a PFS (Personal Financial Specialist) which is a credential given to only a very select few in the country.

A graduate of Purdue University, Bill spent many years in the banking industry before realizing his true passion of helping others achieve financial success. Prior to opening

OnPoint Financial Strategies, Bill worked for and learned from the experts at American Express Financial Advisors; Findlay, Davies & Co.; Hantz Financial Services; and CBIZ Tax and Advisory Services. He also owned and operated a Home Instead Senior Care franchise that provided him with unique insights into the special financial needs and situations of seniors and their families.

Bill makes his home in Scottsdale, AZ with his wife Caren and their dog Daisy. They have 5 children. Bill enjoys playing golf, spending time with his family and traveling the country.

Please feel free to contact Bill at: williamhcantrell@gmail.com.

He would love to hear your feedback and questions.

You may get additional information on estate planning, investments, insurance and other topics by subscribing to his blog at: www.CantrellFinancialStrategies.com

www.ingramcontent.com/pod-product-compliance
Lightning Source LLC
Chambersburg PA
CBHW071225170526
45165CB00003B/988